The River Rescue

by B.G. Hennessy
illustrated by Mena Dolobowsky

MODERN CURRICULUM PRESS
Pearson Learning Group

Saturday was a special day for Roberto and Rosa. Their dad was taking them to the river. They raced to the kitchen.

"Are you ready to go to the river?" asked Dad.

"I hope there are rapids!"
said Roberto.

"There are no rapids on this river.
This is a nice, quiet river," said Dad.

"I hope I catch a shark!" said Rosa.

"There are no sharks in this river.
No rapids, no sharks," said Dad. "Just
peace and quiet."

Mom handed them a cardboard box. "Here's your lunch. Put it by the truck," said Mom.

There was a big pile by the truck.

"Do we need *all* of this?" asked Rosa.

"Yes, now let's pack up!" said Dad.

Mom waved good-by and they
were on their way.

"Who wants to be the navigator?"
asked Dad.

"It depends," said Roberto.

"What does it depend on?"
asked Dad.

"It depends on what a navigator
is!" said Roberto.

Dad laughed. "The navigator tells
me which roads to take. I marked the
way on the map."

"I'll be the navigator," said Roberto.

They rode for a long time.

"Are we there yet?" asked Rosa.

"Roberto, where do I turn?" asked Dad.

"I'm not sure!" said Roberto as he searched the map. "What if we already passed it?"

"We're lost!" cried Rosa.

"No, we're not!" said Roberto. "Make the next right turn, Dad."

At last, they got to the river. "It's bigger than I thought it would be," said Roberto.

"It's so pretty," said Rosa.

"This is perfect," said Dad. "It's quiet and peaceful."

9

"I'm going fishing!" said Rosa.

"I'm going to play in the water!" said Roberto.

"I'm going to watch both of you," said Dad.

"Dad, may we take our tubes out to that little island?" asked Rosa.

"May we take our lunch too?" asked Roberto.

"Fine. Just stay where I can see you," said Dad.

Rosa and Roberto played for a long time. They built a cliff and a castle. They waved to people going by in boats.

"I'm hungry. Let's eat," said Roberto.

13

"Oh, no!" said Roberto. "Our lunch is gone!"

"Oh, no!" said Rosa. "Our tubes are gone!"

"Oh, no! Our way back to shore is gone! We're stranded! DAD!" they called. "HELP!"

"Hold on," he called. "I'm coming!"

Just after they got back to shore they saw a police boat towing three tubes and a cooler.

"Are these tubes yours?" asked the policeman.

"Yes! Thank you!" said Roberto and Rosa.

"Let's eat before our lunch escapes again," said Dad. "Besides, it is almost time to start back home."

POLICE

It was dark when they got home.

"How was your day?" asked Mom.

"It was GREAT!" said Rosa and Roberto. "We almost got lost on the way, we were stranded on an island, and our lunch was rescued by the police!"

"Just a nice, peaceful day on the river!" laughed Dad.